A World of Knowing

A World of Knowing

A Story about Thomas Hopkins Gallaudet

by Andy Russell Bowen
illustrations by Elaine Wadsworth

A Carolrhoda Creative Minds Book

Carolrhoda Books, Inc./Minneapolis

For Sarah, from whom I am always learning

The illustrator wishes to thank Winfield McChord Jr., Executive
Director of the American School for the Deaf, for his assistance
in the preparation of this book.

This book is available in two editions:
Library binding by Carolrhoda Books, Inc.
Soft cover by First Avenue Editions
c/o The Lerner Group
241 First Avenue North, Minneapolis, MN 55401

Library of Congress Cataloging-in-Publication Data

Bowen, Andy Russell.
    A world of knowing : a story about Thomas Hopkins Gallaudet / by
Andy Russell Bowen ; illustrations by Elaine Wadsworth.
        p.   cm. — (A Carolrhoda creative minds book)
    Summary: A biography of the founder of the first school for the deaf in
the United States who, among other accomplishments, evolved a new sign
language and wrote children's books.
    Includes bibliographical references and index.
    ISBN 0-87614-871-2 (lib. bdg.) — ISBN 0-87614-954-9 (pbk.)
    1. Gallaudet, T. H. (Thomas Hopkins), 1787-1851—Juvenile
literature, 2. Teachers of the deaf—United States—Biography—Juvenile
literature. [1. Gallaudet, T. H. (Thomas Hopkins), 1787-1851. 2. Teachers
of the deaf.] I. Wadsworth, Elaine, ill. II. Title. III. Series.
HV2534.G3B69 1995
371.91'2'092—dc20
[B]   95-1900
                                                                   CIP
                                                                    AC

Manufactured in the United States of America

1 2 3 4 5 6 – MA – 00 99 98 97 96 95

Table of Contents

1

An Upping Stone

Thomas Gallaudet's eyes were watering so much he could hardly see through his glasses. He was having trouble catching his breath between coughs. His chest was starting to ache again, and that nagging sting was burning the inside of his nose. He told his friends to go on without him. Thomas was used to being left behind.

In the town of Hartford, Connecticut, where Thomas lived, there were hills to climb, fences to jump, woods to play tag in, and an old woolen mill to explore. But thirteen-year-old Thomas seldom joined in the games and races and adventures. He could never keep up.

Ever since the day of his birth, on December 10, 1787, Thomas had been smaller and weaker than other children his age. There was nothing he could do about it. He was just born that way. Even though he was the oldest of the Gallaudet children, Thomas wore the hand-me-downs of his brother Charles, who was several years younger and a couple of inches taller.

Thomas had a weakness, the doctor explained to the boy's mother. Perhaps if he kept to a good, wholesome diet, he might overcome it someday. But in spite of all the tasty roasts and crusty breads and creamy puddings that Mrs. Gallaudet fed her family, Thomas never grew big and strong.

Thomas accepted his condition. But that didn't mean he liked it very much. He didn't like it when the doctor put an ear to his chest and heard rattling sounds inside. He didn't like lagging behind his friends all the time. He didn't like being different. But he complained only to himself.

Usually when his friends were playing outdoors, Thomas would wander off. "I used to steal away from my companions," he said, "and find out a lonely spot in the fields or woods where we were sporting." He liked to nestle into a comfortable hollow between the roots of an old tree. There he would sit for hours and daydream. Sometimes while his thoughts were in a faraway place, Thomas picked up a stick and drew pictures. "A thousand strange figures in the sand," he called them. Or he whistled a song that his mother sang to him when he was little. All the while, a better life was taking shape in his imagination.

Then at night, in his attic room in the big house on Prospect Street, Thomas sat and wrote in his journal by candlelight. "I used to delight and dwell upon what might be," he remembered later, "and to conjure up such scenes of prosperity for myself and friends and all mankind." Thomas believed that somewhere in those daydreams lay his future.

In spite of Thomas's small size and poor health, people looked up to him. By the time he was fourteen years old, there were eight Gallaudet children. Thomas's brothers and sisters came to him with their problems, and his parents often asked his advice about raising their large family. At school Thomas did well in all his subjects. His teachers said that he was one of their best students, and all of his classmates respected him. It was only in Thomas's own eyes that he didn't measure up.

Thomas fought to balance his physical weakness with a strong will and a sense of purpose. He had inherited these traits, he was told, from his ancestors.

The Gallaudets could trace their family back to civic leaders and clergymen and ambassadors in important cities of Europe. On his mother's side was the Reverend Thomas Hooker, who sailed from England with the early Puritans and founded the town of Hartford in 1636. On his father's side were French Huguenots, a group of Protestants who had fought for religious freedom in France. They were people of stubborn courage and passionate spirit, and they spent their lives doing good deeds. Thomas was determined to carry on the family traditions. When he grew up, he too was going to do something important.

At fourteen Thomas had learned everything the Hartford Grammar School could teach him. Mr. Gallaudet was very proud of Thomas and announced that his eldest son would go to Yale College in New Haven, Connecticut. Founded in the early 1700s, Yale was one of the finest schools in the country. Any bright man would give his right arm to go there. At Yale, thought Thomas, I will have a new life. Some of my dreams will begin to come true.

A few weeks before he was to leave for New Haven, Thomas passed by the Jeremy Addams, an old tavern that served the town as a meeting place and stagecoach terminal. In the stable yard behind the inn, Thomas noticed a spare carriage wheel propped against a hitching post, waiting to be loaded. Huffing and puffing, he coaxed the heavy wheel out of the mud and dragged it toward the waiting coach. Thomas wanted to prove that he could take on the world. But a rude shove knocked him off balance as someone jerked the wheel away from him. He caught a whiff of beery breath and heard the voice of the innkeeper muttering that Thomas couldn't possibly heft the wheel up into the coach. "You're much too short and puny," the voice mocked. "An upping stone is what you'd need . . . to put yourself in square spitting distance of our driver."

Dirty and out of breath, Thomas walked home to his attic room to add another failure to his list. An upping stone indeed! That was what ladies used to step daintily into a coach. "If only feelings could be discarded like boots," Thomas wrote in his diary that night, "and a new set purchased."

It was the fall of 1802, and the day of Thomas's departure finally arrived. Waving good-bye to his family, he climbed into the stagecoach and peered out the open door for one last glimpse of his hometown. Then the dark wood of the carriage walls and the smell of polished leather closed in on him, and the whinnies of the six-horse team signaled the start of his journey down the dusty turnpike to New Haven.

One of the first things Thomas did after he found his room and unpacked his trunk was sit down and acquaint himself with page after page of the *Laws of Yale-College*.

One rule said, "If any scholar shall be absent from any lecture . . . he may be fined three cents." Another warned that if a student went "a-fishing or sailing" without permission, the fine was thirty-four cents. Going to college was very serious business. Most of the time, Thomas managed to stay out of trouble.

Thomas had learned so much at grammar school that he was allowed to enter college as a sophomore. The three years at Yale passed quickly. One day toward the end of his senior year, Thomas was called into the college president's office. He would always remember how nervous he was and how hard he tried not to show it.

President Dwight told Thomas that in spite of his fine record at Yale, someone else had been selected to give the valedictory speech at commencement. As a top student and debater, Thomas was the obvious choice for speaker. But he was only five and a half feet tall, too short to be seen in the back rows of the auditorium. The faculty had chosen instead one of Thomas's classmates, a young man who was four inches taller.

"I'm sure you can understand," President Dwight said. Thomas understood all right. But he wondered whether he would ever get over his disappointment. Maybe he did need an upping stone after all.

②

Finding the Pearl

Thomas graduated from Yale in September of 1805, just two months before his eighteenth birthday. He had one of the best educations the country had to offer. Now he needed a job. But before he looked for work, he had to ask himself what he was going to do with his life. Answering this question proved to be harder than he thought.

Over the next few years, Thomas tried several different jobs. The first two started out well and promised a good future. But each time his old enemy, poor health, got in the way. One job was with an important law firm in Hartford. Thomas had all the makings of a good lawyer. He was quick to understand what a law meant and how it applied to the matter before him. He talked easily to clients and they liked his openness and honesty. There was only one thing wrong. Some of the other lawyers in the firm were pipe smokers. After months of coughing his way through clouds of tobacco smoke, Thomas finally had to quit.

His next position was as a tutor at Yale. Thomas was happy to be back in familiar surroundings, but his cough still bothered him. Doctors told him to spend more time outdoors, where the fresh air would soothe his lungs and make his breathing easier. Thomas knew that he must restore his health before he did anything else, so once again he resigned. His dreams of doing something important would just have to wait.

Sometimes it seemed to Thomas that his life was moving backward instead of forward. To make things worse, he believed that he had fallen into some bad habits. Ashamed of enjoying himself too much at a party, Thomas vowed he would give up dancing and other such merrymaking for the rest of his life. "I am languid, and cold, and slothful," he complained. He thought that he was insincere and proud and vain as well. No one could be harder on Thomas than Thomas himself.

Around this time, he heard about a job with a company that made everything from tools to trinkets. They needed a door-to-door salesman in the backwoods of Kentucky and Ohio. The only way to travel from place to place was on foot or horseback. Thomas took the job.

Country lanes and remote farmhouses were a welcome change from the noise of towns and the stale air of offices. When he knocked on a door ready to peddle his wares, Thomas looked like a friendly elf in a fairy tale, with a big smile on his face and a bag of surprises slung over one shoulder. It was only a matter of seconds before the children of the family were crowding onto the bare floor around his feet, impatient to see what was in the bag. There might be a handful of colored ribbons to tie up a girl's hair, or a satin bow to dress up her well-patched pinafore. There was always a jackknife for a boy who liked to pry and peel and whittle. The heavy lump at the bottom of Thomas's sack might be a shiny new cook pot for the lady of the house or a gold-trimmed clock for the corner shelf.

Most of the families Thomas visited were very poor. They raised their own chickens, grew their own vegetables, built their own cabins, and sewed their own clothes. They had only enough coins put away in the sugar jar to buy one or two small items. Thomas could never resist giving away a little something to each of the children—a set of brass buttons or a spool of silk thread.

Thomas wondered why so many of the children he met weren't in school. There's no teacher, they often explained. Perhaps their last one had come from Philadelphia or Boston and didn't like living in a shack in the woods. It would be a while before they could find another one. Very well then, thought Thomas, I will teach them myself.

Thomas told the children stories from the Bible and tales of the early New England settlers. He drew maps of the seventeen states and showed the children where they themselves lived. He made sure they could name the four presidents in order: George Washington, John Adams, Thomas Jefferson, and James Madison.

One time, calling on a family who lived far from an inn or lodging house, Thomas was invited to spend the night. The children curled up in blankets on the floor, letting their visitor sleep in comfort on the feather bed. Thomas lay awake for a long time, listening to the quiet rhythm of the new clock. He had logged a year of door-to-door selling in the pages of his journal. Time was ticking away, and he hadn't yet found the really important thing that he was going to do with his life.

When he awoke the next morning to the smell of smoked bacon and corn pone, Thomas thought of a story that his father used to tell him. It was a parable from the Bible, and he could still remember the words. "The kingdom of heaven is like unto a merchant man seeking a goodly pearl," it said, "who, when he had found one pearl of great price, went and sold all that he had, and bought it."

Somewhere out there was Thomas's pearl—his life's work, his special mission—waiting to be discovered. Thomas was tired of thinking about the things he couldn't do because of poor health. From now on, he wasn't going to worry about what was. He was going to dream of what might be.

During the winter of 1812, Thomas finally decided what he wanted to do. He was going into the ministry, where he could teach people and help them to find a better way of life. He studied for two years at Andover College in Massachusetts and earned his divinity degree. He was offered a church of his own in

Portsmouth, New Hampshire, but he didn't have the strength for such a demanding job. Instead, Thomas settled for second best and became a traveling preacher, filling in wherever he was needed. This way, he was able to work when he felt strong enough and rest when he had to.

Whenever he could, Thomas returned to Hartford to stay with his family. One beautiful summer day he was resting on the front steps of the house on Prospect Street. He closed his eyes for a quick nap and drifted off into a daydream. A moment later he was jarred awake by the sound of children laughing.

Down the street he saw Teddy, the youngest of his nine brothers and sisters. Dressed for play in summer britches, Teddy was in the midst of a game of hide-and-seek, ducking and darting and shouting with his friends. Then Thomas noticed a little girl standing apart from the other children. She didn't look as if she had been playing. Her long, yellow curls lay neatly in place, and the ruffles of her starched pinafore were still freshly ironed. Thomas guessed that she must be about nine years old. How well he remembered himself at that age, standing outside the circle of children, watching the games he couldn't play. Why didn't she join in? he wondered. There didn't seem to be anything wrong with her.

Thomas waved to Teddy, calling him away from the game. Who was the little girl? he wanted to know, and why wasn't she playing? Teddy explained that she was the daughter of Dr. Cogswell, who lived down the street. She was unable to hear or speak, so she didn't play with the other children. She didn't go to school with them either, because no one could teach her to read or write. She didn't even know her own name.

And so it was that Thomas first saw Alice Cogswell. He didn't know it yet, because the idea hadn't quite begun to take shape in his mind. But in finding Alice, Thomas had found his pearl.

③

A Silent Prison

Mason Cogswell was one of Hartford's best doctors, but he was practicing medicine long before the discovery of vaccines that could prevent many childhood diseases. His daughter Alice came down with a case of spotted fever when she was only two. Alice recovered, but as sometimes happened with spotted fever, she began to grow deaf. Unable to hear other people speaking, she soon forgot the sounds that she had known before her illness. Within two years, Alice had lost both her hearing and her speech.

The Cogswells tried to help Alice understand what they were saying to her. They tried to guess what she wanted to say to them. But they just didn't know how to communicate with someone who could neither hear nor speak. No one else knew either.

By the time Thomas first saw Alice, she had been living in a world of total silence for five years. As a child he had known what it felt like to be left out. But at least he could hear and understand the world around him. When Alice watched the other children playing, their arms waving and their mouths going at full speed, there was no sound to tell her what they were laughing and shouting about. When she sat under a tree to rest, she couldn't hear a gnat whining around her head or leaves getting restless before a storm. A life of just watching wasn't much fun for Alice to look forward to. How lonely she must be.

Thomas remembered a young boy he had seen the year before, a deaf child about Alice's age. Two men were making fun of the child, calling him names like "dummy" and "dog." The more scared and helpless the boy looked, the crueler the men were to him. Thomas didn't want this to happen to Alice.

He got up from his step and walked slowly toward the little girl, taking care not to startle her. He picked one of the purple violets that sprouted wild in the grass and offered it to Alice. She didn't seem to be at all afraid. Maybe she guessed that Thomas liked children. Maybe she sensed that he too felt different.

Thomas was dressed as gentlemen usually were in those days, in a tailored suit and a boxy gray top hat. Just for fun, he took off his hat and put it on Alice's head. She looked at Thomas and waited to see what he would do next. An idea was starting to come to him. "I wonder if I could, if she could . . . " And before the thought was even finished, he stooped down to pick up a stick. Making sure that Alice was paying attention, Thomas reached out, took the hat, and set it on the ground between them. With the stick he wrote the letters *H A T* in the dirt next to the hat.

Alice let out a high squeak. Thomas supposed it was laughter. She was having fun. That was a good start. Once again he pointed to the hat on the ground and retraced the letters *H A T* with his writing stick. Alice found all this very entertaining. She wanted to play too. While Thomas watched, she fluttered her hands in the air and scuffed her shoes in the dirt, squeaking cheerfully all the while.

Thomas went along with Alice's little game of trading tricks. He smiled his approval when she came up with new ones, like throwing a stone or pulling on one of her curls. He was glad that Alice was enjoying herself, but how could he let her know that he was trying to teach her something?

Thomas lost track of how long he'd been standing there pointing to the hat and scratching *H A T* deeper into the dirt. He was thinking about giving up, when all of a sudden, Alice snatched the hat from the ground, plopped it back on her head, and waved her finger at the three letters.

Thomas would never know exactly what was going on in Alice's mind. All that mattered to him was that she had made a connection between the object on her head and the writing in the dust. Alice had learned her first word.

At the end of a long day Thomas was usually exhausted, but today he felt stronger than ever. He lifted Alice up into his arms and hugged her. The hat flew off her head and fell at his feet. Alice pointed to the hat, then to the letters *H A T*. They both laughed. The doors of Alice's silent prison had opened.

④
Another Language

A lot happened in the next few days. Alice learned her second word, *A L I C E.* Dr. Cogswell began to think, to hope, that Thomas held the key to his daughter's future. And Thomas decided that he had a great deal to learn before he could start teaching Alice in earnest.

He began to spend more and more time in Dr. Cogswell's library, browsing through heavy volumes on medicine and history and science, looking for anything that might help him to understand deafness.

Like Dr. Cogswell, he knew there was nothing wrong with Alice's mind. She seemed to be just as intelligent as other children her age. But people called her "dummy" because she couldn't hear or speak.

Over the last few years, Dr. Cogswell too had read everything he could find about deafness. All through history, deaf people had been misunderstood, he told Thomas. They were often thought to be retarded or less than human. Doctors had never understood what caused deafness or how it might be cured.

Just recently in France, a physician named Jean-Marc Itard had been experimenting on deaf patients, hoping to stumble onto a treatment. He tried pouring a mixture of sea salt, wine, horseradish, rose petals, and wild ginger into the ears of deaf children. It didn't help. He tried pushing a sharp instrument into a patient's nose and then shooting fluid through the Eustachian tube, which leads to the ear. This procedure, which Itard performed on over a hundred children, didn't seem to work either, and it was very painful. He decided to try one last experiment, hoping to jar his patients back to their senses. With a hammer, he struck a blow to the skulls of several children, just behind the ear. This too failed, and Dr. Itard gave up entirely. "Medicine does not work on the dead," he concluded, "and as far as I am concerned, the ear is dead in the deaf-mute. There is nothing for science to do about it."

Educators hadn't done much to help either. There were no schools for the deaf in the United States and only a few in Europe. Some people traveled abroad to go to those schools, but the Cogswells thought Alice was much too young to be so far away from home.

As Thomas worked his way through Dr. Cogswell's books, he learned that in European schools the deaf were taught to communicate in two very different ways. One way concentrated on reading lips and learning to speak out loud. This was called the oral method. With the other method, called sign, deaf people used their hands to speak. They spelled out words in the air, shaping their fingers to form the letters of the alphabet. Sometimes they acted out entire phrases or feelings.

The book that impressed Thomas the most was written by the Abbé Sicard, a priest who taught the sign method of communication to deaf children in Paris. Thomas had learned a little French at Yale and began at once to study the words and pictures in Sicard's book. He soon found that by adding some of their own signs to the French ones, he and Alice could talk together. If he wanted to tell her, for example, that the lady next door had a new baby, all he had to do was point to the neighbor's house and rock an imaginary child in his arms. "Is it a girl?"Alice might ask, pulling on the ribbons of a make-believe bonnet tied beneath her chin. "No, it's a boy," Thomas could answer, touching the brim of a pretend hat on his head.

From that time on, Thomas seldom had a day off. He traveled as a preacher on weekends and spent every weekday with Alice. Over the months that Dr. Cogswell watched his daughter and her teacher working together, an idea began to grow in his mind. Why not start a school for deaf children right here in Hartford, so that others like Alice could learn too? Dr. Cogswell had read that there were hundreds, maybe even thousands of people across the country who couldn't hear or speak. In his own state of Connecticut, there were over eighty people who were deaf. Many of them were just as smart and eager to learn as Alice. But without special teachers and schools, each one lived alone in a silent world, unable to communicate with anyone else.

Dr. Cogswell knew that he couldn't start a school all by himself. He would have to find other people to help him raise money for classrooms and books and teachers. He would have to travel all around New

England to let everyone know about his school. A lot of hard work lay ahead, and Dr. Cogswell knew just where he would begin.

On the evening of April 13, 1815, Dr. Cogswell invited eight friends to meet at his house. He wanted to talk to them about his idea. He also invited Thomas, who was to tell the other guests about Alice. Doing his best to persuade them, Thomas assured the gentlemen seated before him that deaf children were just as intelligent as hearing children. He told them how excited his own pupil had been to learn *H A T* and *A L I C E.*

Thomas was doing his job well, but if anyone could convince these men, it was Alice herself. Dr. Cogswell left the room and returned a moment later with his daughter. Then, in the special language that they had been practicing every day, Thomas asked Alice if she liked learning all the new things he was teaching her. With quick fingers, she pointed to herself, drew a circle in the air, and touched her forehead. She was saying, explained Thomas, "I always want understand."

Before the evening ended, Thomas taught Dr. Cogswell's guests their first word in the language of the deaf. Clapping their hands together twice, they said the word *school.*

The next morning Dr. Cogswell and his friends formed themselves into a committee and agreed to raise money to educate deaf children. By the end of the day, they had opened a special account at the Bank of Hartford.

When the townspeople heard about the school, some promised to help. Many of them had watched Alice and her teacher parading down Hartford's main street, laughing and signing to each other, fingers dancing in the air. They looked like a couple of pied pipers, with Thomas's younger brothers and sisters signing in a long train behind them. Others, who had seen Alice crying from exhaustion, clucked their tongues and said that trying to teach deaf people was a waste of time.

A few days after the meeting, Dr. Cogswell and his committee chose Thomas Gallaudet to be the principal of the new school. They would raise enough money to send him to Europe, where he could learn firsthand the teaching methods that he had read so much about.

Still a young man in his twenties, Thomas was to be the head of America's first school for the deaf. What an honor. And what a responsibility. He worried that his poor health might stand in the way. But, he decided, if others believed he could do the job, then he had better start believing it too. Six weeks later, Thomas sailed for Europe. In his brand-new passport was a written entry describing him as five feet six inches tall, with dark eyes, a straight nose, large lips, and prominent teeth.

The Atlantic crossing to Liverpool took one month. From there Thomas went on to London to visit the Asylum for the Deaf and Dumb. He had heard that this school was the best of its kind in Europe. He couldn't wait to start learning from the students and their teachers.

Thomas's heart sank when he was met at the door by several stern, unfriendly men dressed in formal velvet robes. He soon learned that the asylum was owned by a family named Braidwood. So were all the other schools for the deaf in England. The Braidwoods were powerful, secretive, and selfish. They made a good living teaching the deaf and didn't want outsiders like Thomas to start schools that might compete with their own. The teachers at the asylum refused to let Thomas visit their classes or observe their methods. The children he saw in the halls looked frightened and unhappy.

Thomas decided to give up on the English schools and sail across the channel to France. He was going to visit the Royal Institution for the Deaf and Dumb.

There he would meet the Abbé Sicard, the priest whose book had taught him so much about sign language.

The Royal Institution was everything Thomas had hoped for. He was invited into the classrooms, where children were signing back and forth as fast as their minds and hands would let them. He soon became good friends with one of the teachers, a deaf priest named Laurent Clerc.

During the days, Thomas visited Clerc's classes. After school the two men would sit and sign together well into the night. As a young student, Clerc told Thomas, he had tried to lip-read and to speak a few words out loud. But when his teacher slapped him for mispronouncing a word, Clerc decided he would never speak again. It is very difficult for deaf people to imitate sounds they've never heard, he explained to Thomas. And it's often hard for hearing people to understand what deaf people are saying. With sign language, both the deaf and the hearing can communicate clearly.

On a warm June day, when Thomas had been in Europe for over a year, a letter came from Alice, who was still being privately tutored. "This morning study all in school away Geography all beautiful," it said. " . . . Come back little while—O all very glad, O beautiful—I love you very much—Your affectionate, Alice Cogswell."

Thomas knew it was time to go home. He walked to a shipping agent and, with the little money he had left, bought two tickets to New York. One was for himself. The other was for Laurent Clerc, who was going with Thomas to teach at the new school.

⑤

Knowing and Knowing

Hartford's school for deaf children was scheduled to open on April 15, 1817. For Thomas, opening day would mark the real beginning of his life's work. For Alice, the first day would open a world of magic, a world of "knowing and knowing," she said, "knowing without end."

For Dr. Cogswell and his committee, now the board of directors of the new school, the fast-approaching day called for a flurry of decisions. It was their job to figure out where the classrooms and sleeping quarters should be located and what subjects should be taught. And of course the school must have a name. They voted to call it the Connecticut Asylum for the Education and Instruction of Deaf and Dumb Persons.

What a terrible choice, Thomas thought. The name was too long and too hard to remember. And the words *dumb* and *asylum* made it sound like a place for stupid or insane people. Thomas didn't like the location the board chose either, a few rented rooms in a dingy old building on Prospect Street. But he couldn't take time to worry about all that. He had too much else to do.

Thomas set to work, scrubbing and painting the dreary classrooms. One day when the paint smell made him feel sick, he went outside. As he walked down the street, enjoying the fresh air of early spring, he thought about the children who were coming to his school. Deaf children knew very little about the world outside their own families. Many of them were leaving home for the first time. Everything and everyone would be strange and frightening to them.

As Thomas strolled past the Jeremy Addams Tavern, he remembered the sounds and smells of the stagecoach that first carried him to New Haven. He remembered how excited he had been to be going away to school, to be starting a new life. Soon Thomas's own pupils would see their lives beginning to change. They would learn to read and write and talk to each other in their new language. They would stop feeling inadequate and isolated. Each one of them would leave a world of emptiness and enter a land of knowing.

In the months before opening day, Thomas traveled around New England talking with families of deaf children and telling them about the school. Alice was now fourteen and old enough, Thomas thought, to go with him on some of his shorter trips. One day he took her on a visit to the Fowler farm to meet Sophia and Parnell. The Fowler sisters, ages nineteen and twenty, were deaf and didn't speak or sign. They lived with their parents.

Alice and Thomas were invited to stay for dinner before the horse-and-buggy ride back to Hartford. After the meal Mr. Fowler used a few simple signs of his own to try to tell his daughters about Thomas's school. Sophia began to hop around in circles, setting her black curls bouncing. Then she looked at Thomas, smiling and touching her forehead. All of a sudden, Alice began signing to her teacher, fingers flying. "She guesses at going someplace to learn. She guesses that you teach knowing and knowing."

On opening day, there were eight students: Alice, the Fowler sisters, and five others. Joseph, age eleven, was happy the moment he walked in the door. He slid down banisters and ran up stairs. He poked his nose everywhere and played with everything he could get his hands on. Ten-year-old George was homesick and couldn't stop crying. Another boy, thirteen, was so scared that he rolled into a ball like a hedgehog and refused to budge. The oldest student was a fifty-one-year-old artist named Joseph Brewster.

The most frightened of all was ten-year-old Julia. Both deaf and blind, she didn't understand where she was or what was happening. For the first few days, Julia screamed most of the time and wouldn't let anyone near her. But little by little she came to trust Laurent Clerc. After a while, she let him lead her by the hand from place to place. Before long Julia was learning the alphabet, her fingertips tracing the letters that Thomas had carved on a big wooden board. Next Julia learned to sign, by placing her hands on Thomas's and copying the movements of his fingers. Within a few weeks, she was starting to sew. She held the end of the thread between her teeth and coaxed it through the eye of the needle with the tip of her tongue. Then her fingers guided the stitches in a straight line.

In the first few days of school, Thomas taught his pupils to sign two very important words, *tears* and *smiles*. He told them that these were more than just words. They were feelings common to everyone. Gradually the students began to feel safe. Strange rooms and faces became familiar. They could understand what their teachers said to them, and they could speak for themselves. Tired fingers soon grew strong and skilled at signing.

News of the school spread, and by the end of the first winter there were almost thirty students. Thomas, said his friend Laurent Clerc, had enough work to keep eleven people busy. He taught six classes every day. He showed new teachers how to do their jobs. He ordered pencils and paper and chalkboards. He answered all the letters written to the school asking questions or criticizing or congratulating. When visitors came, he showed them around. He spoke with legislators all over New England, asking them for money to buy supplies and pay teachers.

By the spring of 1818, Thomas had been running the school for a year. He was exhausted. His chest ached, his throat burned, and his eyes watered. "Alas how my energy is gone," he wrote in his diary. One day when Thomas was especially tired, Sophia Fowler gently patted his shoulder. "Are you sick?" she signed. Thomas wondered how such a small thing could make him feel so much better.

Along with everything else he did that first year, Thomas continued to learn more and more about communicating with the deaf. "The language of sign," he realized, "is not to be learned from books. It must be learned . . . from the living, looking, acting model." Along with Laurent Clerc, Thomas was combining the French method of signing with the new signs and facial expressions that his students used. Together, teachers and pupils were creating an American sign language, one that fit their own special needs and reflected their own lives and thoughts.

Just before the end of the year, Thomas received an important message from Washington. James Monroe, president of the United States, wanted to visit the school. In a bustle of excitement, volunteers built a speaker's platform in the street and dressed it up with flags and banners of red, white, and blue. The students, wearing matching ribbons, were to share the platform and the limelight with the president.

On the appointed day, a crowd gathered. Thomas and Laurent Clerc stood ready to escort their honored guest to the speaker's chair. The students prepared to salute. Someone shouted that the president's carriage was approaching.

A tall, stoop-shouldered man stepped down from the coach. On his head was a tricorn hat. It was big and black, with a wide brim that folded up in three places, forming points that stuck up like horns. President Monroe climbed the steps of the speaker's platform and turned to address the audience. He congratulated Thomas and the students on their important work. They had much to be proud of, he told them. He promised that with the help of the United States government, each and every state would soon have a public school for deaf children.

Then President Monroe stepped aside, giving Thomas the speaker's place. Thomas talked about the history of signing, and he showed the president a few words. Next it was the students' turn to greet their guest. Holding their hands above their heads, they moved their fingers to describe the shape of his tricorn hat. They were adding the word *president* to American Sign Language.

Summer vacation came at last. Thomas was looking forward to a good, long rest. He watched from the front steps of the school as each of his pupils waved good-bye. Thomas knew he would miss them all. But more than any of the others, he would miss Sophia Fowler. Earlier that day, she and Parnell had climbed into their father's wagon to jog down the road back to the Fowler farm. "It's summer," Sophia signed to Thomas. "I write you. Letter. You answer?"

"I will answer," Thomas signed back. "I promise. Happy summer, Sophia."

⑥

A Man of Stature

In the next few years, the school grew to well over a hundred students. Important people came to visit— American statesmen Henry Clay and Andrew Jackson and the famous English author Charles Dickens. The United States Congress granted the school a large piece of land for a new three-story building to house classrooms, carpentry workshops, a library, and a dormitory. To Thomas's great relief, the school board decided on a new name, the American School for the Deaf. More teachers were hired and trained, and classes were added in history, religion, and geography. Daily outdoor exercise became a requirement. Thomas was going to prove to the rest of the world that the deaf could be just as independent and productive as the hearing. "All the children of silence must be taught to sing their own song," he said.

With all the duties of a school principal, Thomas had very little time to himself. But one summer day after classes were over, he sat down to do something that had been on his mind for a long time. He was going to compose a letter, the most difficult one he had ever written. It was to be a proposal of marriage to Miss Sophia Fowler.

Thomas had tried not to fall in love with Sophia. How could she possibly feel the same about him? He was thirty-four and she was only twenty-three. He was plain and frail and easily tired. She was pretty and healthy and bouncing with energy. A "rare and radiant maiden," Thomas called her. But he couldn't let another summer go by without letting Sophia know that he wanted to marry her. As luck would have it, Sophia loved Thomas too. A few months later, in August of 1821, they were married.

The following year, Thomas and Sophia had their first child, little Thomas. Sophia was afraid he might be deaf. When the baby was only a few weeks old, she put him to the test. She waited until little Thomas was sound asleep. Then she carried a heavy teakettle from the kitchen and dropped it on the floor next to the baby's cradle. Two startled eyes flew open and little Thomas began to cry. "The baby hears," Sophia signed to her husband. "The baby is not deaf." Over the next fifteen years, there were seven more children, Sophia, Peter, Jane, William, Catherine, Alice, and Edward. Each one of them passed the teakettle test.

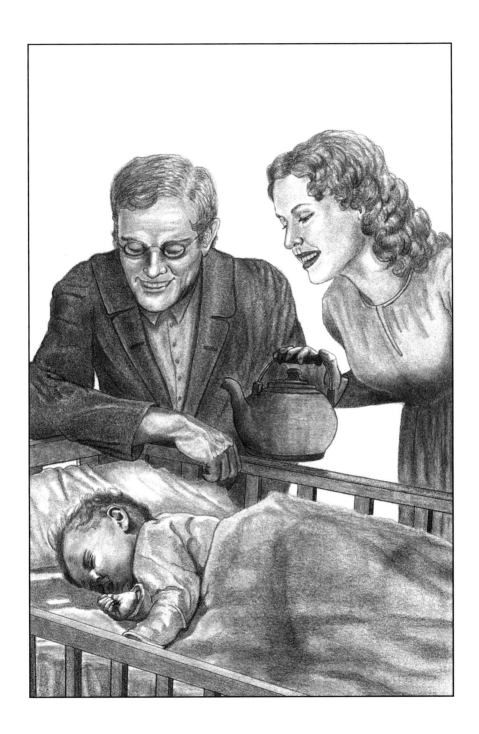

Thomas remained devoted to his work. But there were other important things he wanted to do, and he could never find enough time or strength for all of them. Finally in 1831, after thirteen years as principal of the American School for the Deaf, he decided to resign.

During the time that Thomas was head of the school, the board of directors hadn't always treated him very well. Although he worked harder than anyone else, they paid him less than his teachers earned. They complained when he asked for money to buy things the school needed. And once, they even tried to fire him because he didn't agree with them. But when the board heard of Thomas's decision to leave, they said that no one could ever take his place. His old friend Laurent Clerc cried. His students began to follow him everywhere. "I can see him now," one of them remembered years later, "with a serious face yet a twinkle in his eye." Like so many others, she knew that Thomas was far ahead of his time. "Only his genius," she said, "could have led even children themselves to feel that education is a priceless thing."

As soon as the news spread outside Hartford, Thomas was in great demand. All around the United States, schools for the deaf were springing up, based on his work. He was invited to speak at the country's first teachers' convention. High schools and colleges everywhere wanted to hire him. He was asked to start schools for the blind as he had for the deaf. There were so many choices. Thomas was only forty-three years old. He had made one dream a reality. Now it was time to follow other dreams.

Afterword

Since childhood Thomas had believed that people who felt left out or different had a special kind of understanding for each other. Whether they were deaf or blind or sickly like himself, they should be treated with kindness, not made to feel even more alone. So it wasn't surprising that after he left the school, Thomas kept on looking for others in need, people he could help to lead a better life. When he was offered two jobs as a minister, one at the city jail and the other at the Hartford Retreat for the Insane, he decided to take them both.

Thomas was very busy with two jobs and a large

family. But whenever he had a spare moment, he liked to sit alone in the privacy of his study. It reminded him of the attic room he had shared with his brother Charles. With his head full of his own childhood, Thomas settled down to his favorite pastime, writing books for children. He especially liked retelling stories from the Bible in words that young people could easily understand.

When Thomas was in his early sixties, his former students planned a special day to honor the teacher who had started America's first school for the deaf thirty-three years before. The governor of Connecticut came to the celebration, along with hundreds of Hartford's citizens.

Thomas greeted the crowd, signing to his students, "I rejoice to meet you once more." He would always think of them, he said, with a father's love. As one of the students stood to address the audience, Thomas drifted off into his own thoughts. Thirty-three years and so many changes. The little town of Hartford was now a major city. Along with the old woolen mill, there was a paper mill, a tool manufacturer, a munitions plant, and two newspapers. Train tracks ran past the Jeremy Addams Tavern, replacing the well-worn ruts of the old coach wheels.

In the year that followed, Thomas suffered more

than ever from the condition that had plagued him since childhood. He was too weak to get out of bed, and he ached everywhere. As he lay in his room, Thomas remembered once again the first time he rode off to Yale in the old stagecoach, snatching one more look at Main Street to fix it in his memory. He had the same feeling now, as if he were seeing all the old, familiar things for the last time. On September 10, 1851, at the age of sixty-three, Thomas died.

Several years later, a monument designed by two of Thomas's former students was unveiled on the front lawn of the American School for the Deaf. It was dedicated to the memory of Thomas Hopkins Gallaudet, the inscription read, "by the deaf and dumb of the United States, as a testimonial of profound gratitude to their earliest and best friend and benefactor."

In 1857 Edward Gallaudet, the youngest son of Thomas and Sophia, became superintendent of the new Columbia Institution for the Deaf and Dumb in Washington, D.C. In 1864 President Lincoln signed a proclamation changing the name of the Columbia Institution to the National Deaf-Mute College. Edward Gallaudet was now its president. In following years the name of the school was again changed, first to Gallaudet College and finally to Gallaudet University, in honor of Edward's father.

Still standing outside the main buildings on the Gallaudet campus, there is a statue by the famous American sculptor Daniel Chester French. It is a likeness of Thomas as a young teacher, holding Alice Cogswell on his lap and showing her how to sign the letter *A*. The statue reminds all who see it of Thomas Hopkins Gallaudet, the teacher and friend who led so many children of silence into a land of knowing.

American Manual Alphabet

The American manual alphabet, which is also called finger signing, is one method of communication used by people who are deaf or hearing impaired. Each letter of the alphabet has its own sign, which can be combined with other letter signs to spell out words. People often use finger signing in combination with American Sign Language, a communication method in which a gesture represents an entire idea rather than a letter.

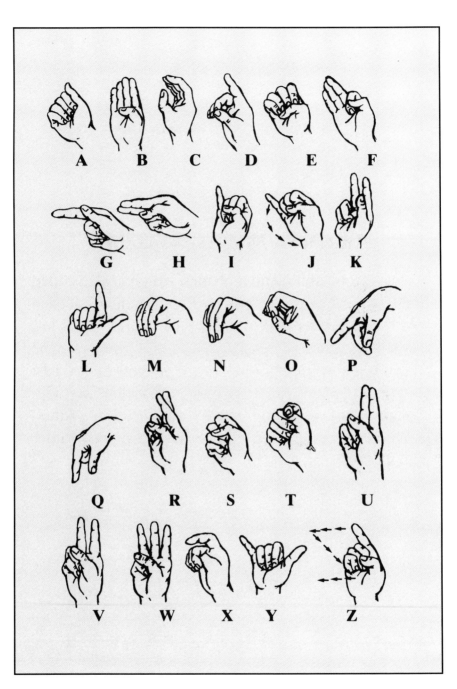

Bibliography

Benderly, Beryl Lieff. *Dancing without Music: Deafness in America.* Washington, D.C.: Gallaudet University Press, 1990.

Boatner, Maxine Tull. *Voice of the Deaf.* Washington, D.C.: Public Affairs Press, 1959.

Butterworth, R. R., and Mickey Flodin. *The Perigee Visual Dictionary of Signing.* New York: Putnam, 1983.

Flodin, Mickey. *Signing for Kids.* New York: Putnam, 1991.

Gallaudet, Edward Miner. *History of the College for the Deaf.* Washington, D.C.: Gallaudet College Press, 1893.

Gallaudet, Edward Miner. *Life of Thomas Hopkins Gallaudet.* New York: Henry Holt, 1888.

Higher Education of the Deaf. Washington, D.C.: Gallaudet College Press, 1954.

Lane, Harlan. *When the Mind Hears, A History of the Deaf.* New York: Random House, 1984.

Neimark, Anne E. *A Deaf Child Listened: Thomas Gallaudet, Pioneer in American Education.* New York: William Morrow, 1983.

Sullivan, M. B., and Linda Bourke. *A Show of Hands.* New York: Harper & Row, 1985.

Yale-College President and Fellows. *The Laws of Yale-College.* New Haven: Thomas Green and Son, 1800.

Index